Ride Lake Superior

By Cynthia Lueck Sowden

© 2015, Cynthia Lueck Sowden

Cover and book design by Lisa Marek, Fat Cat Art Studio

First Edition

ISBN: 1517462711

ISBN-13: 978-1517462710

Table of Contents

Introduction

My husband, Ralph, and I rode the Lake Superior Circle in the summer of 2013. As road trips go, it's not a long ride. Some riders complete the entire loop around the lake in a day or two. But there's a lot to see and do along the way. Take time to enjoy the journey!

Road conditions may have changed for better or for worse since we rode the circle, but I'm sure the places and things you'll see along the route are just as interesting now as they were then.

- Cynthia Lueck Sowden
August 2015

For Arlene, who always wants to hear about our latest trip.

STOP
ARRÊT

STOP PROCEED WHEN LANE IS CLEAR
ARRETEZ AVANCEZ LORSQUE LA VOIE EST LIBRE

Getting into Canada isn't as easy as it used to be.

Before You Go

If you're thinking about embarking on a ride around Lake Superior, here are a few tips.

The Lake Superior Circle Route

A word of warning: The "official" Lake Superior Circle Route (the one designated by highway signs) does not always follow along the lake shore. In Michigan, for instance, the route runs from Ironwood to Marquette along Michigan 28 and US 41. If you want to try to keep the lake in view as we did, you'll have to take the so-called "connecting" roads.

Visit **www.ridelakesuperior.com**. It's a website devoted to touring Lake Superior via motorcycle. It provides maps, a list of iTunes and things to see, from Winnie the Pooh Park in White River, Ontario, to Split Rock Lighthouse in Minnesota.

The Lake Superior Travel Guide is another good resource. It's $9.95, and you can order it online at **http://www.lakesuperiortravel-guide.com**.

We wanted to ride some additional routes in Minnesota after our circle, so we rode the route counter clockwise. You may want to ride it clockwise.

Your Passport: Don't Leave Home without It

The days of freely crossing the border into Canada are gone. You will need your passport to ride into Canada and you will need it to re-enter the United States. A driver's license won't do.

Make sure your passport is up-to-date well before you put the kickstand up. Getting a passport is not as easy as it was pre-9/11. It also takes longer to process and is more expensive.

You may wish to apply for an enhanced driver's license (EDL), which can be used in lieu of a passport. An EDL may be issued by a state or provincial government as part of the Western Hemisphere Travel Initiative, which is supposed to streamline cross-border land or water travel between the U.S. and Canada. Minnesota, New York, Vermont, Washington and Michigan issue EDLs. Ontario issues EDLs to licensed Canadian drivers who reside in Ontario.

Expect delays at the border crossings. When we entered Canada at Sault Ste. Marie, Ralph was questioned closely about his activities in Amsterdam (he had traveled through there during a business trip to Austria). When we re-entered the States at the U.S. Customs station just north of Grand Portage, Minnesota, we were stopped and our baggage searched. Ralph's motorcycle maintenance tools were inspected closely.

Border crossing personnel are touchy about photos, too. Although I grabbed a shot of the lineup at Sault Ste. Marie, a large sign on the U.S. side in Minnesota said, "NO PHOTOS."

Helmet Laws

Minnesota, Wisconsin and Michigan have "partial" helmet laws. In Minnesota, all riders under 18 years of age or riders in training must wear a helmet. The same is true for Wisconsin. In Michigan, riders under 21 or riders who are not insured are required to wear a helmet. All Canadian provinces require a motorcycle helmet for rider and passenger. Period.

Firearms

Some bikers like to carry a firearm. Generally, most of the firearms transport rules concerning the U.S. and Canada cover hunting rifles and shotguns.

Canada will allow you to bring handgun into the country if you procure an Authorization to Transport (ATT) permit in advance. You will have to fill out a Firearms Declaration form (you can download it from the Royal Canadian Mounted Police website, www. http://www.rcmp-grc.gc.ca), but don't sign it until you're in front of a Canadian customs officer. You will have to pay a fee ($50 at this writing), and it will be good for 60 days.

On the U.S. side of the border, you should file electronic export information (EEI) with the Department of State. You will want to obtain a form called CBP4457 which allows you to take the gun and its ammunition into Canada and return to the U.S. This form is meant to streamline your re-entry into the country, but be prepared to declare your guns and ammo at the border. Visit **https://help.cpb.gov** for more information.

Unless you're going to hunt caribou, you may want to skip the bureaucratic hassle and leave your weapon at home.

Bring Warm Clothes

Canada's motorcycling season is short — roughly May to October. Extra hoodies and even long underwear can come in handy, especially when you're near Lake Superior. We rode the Circle in August, and temperatures hovered in the fifties for much of the trip.

Be prepared to run into foggy conditions anywhere around Lake Superior.

Foggy weather occurs frequently along the lake. Be prepared to run into areas of poor visibility, especially as you travel closer to the lake.

Bring a Gas Can

If you plan to leave the main highway, extra gas might be a good idea.

Although we encountered no problems getting gas for our bike, we did notice that some Canadian bikers carried gas cans with them. If you plan to travel away from the Trans-Canada Highway, carrying some extra fuel might be a good idea. If you do plan to bring gas with you from the U.S., be sure to declare it at the border. By the way, the Imperial Gallon is no more; gas is sold by the liter in Canada.

Road Conditions

The Trans-Canada Highway is well maintained from Sault St. Marie to Thunder Bay. It's a four-lane highway in many places, two lanes in others, but there's not much traffic. We experienced some road work closer to Thunder Bay, but it didn't disrupt traffic. Highway maintenance is some-what poorer on the U.S. side, with Minnesota and Wisconsin leading the way in terms of lousy road upkeep.

Wildlife

You can expect to see all kinds of critters on the road, some of them living. The area around Lake Superior is prime deer and moose habitat. Moose crossing signs are fairly common along the Trans-Canada Highway.

No Cell Service

Lake Superior is a big, beautiful expanse of – nothing. Even if you arrange for international cell phone service before you enter Canada, be aware that your cell phone may not work in many places along the lake. Although you'll get good reception in larger places like Houghton, Michigan, there just aren't that many transmission towers near the "shining Big-Sea-Water."

Moose are a wildlife hazard in Canada.

Book Early

Normally, we travel without making hotel reservations, preferring to stop when we're tired and not push ourselves to make a certain destination. For this trip, however, we called ahead. This was especially important in Ontario, where towns and hotels are few and far between. Many were filled two months in advance.

Don't be fooled by what you see on the Internet, either. A hotel we had passed over in Terrace Bay actually looked better than its photo and was across the highway from Lake Superior. The motel we chose in Nipigon was far from downtown and the lake. The nearest restaurant was the BP station down the highway and the food was indifferently cooked and served. They know a captive audience when they see one.

You will get what you pay for in terms of hotel rooms. We made a conscious decision to stay at mom-and-pop motels along the lake (to recall the places we stayed at during family vacations in our youth) and had no complaints. The beds took up most of the room and the bathrooms were small. But the owners were great, and provided rags for wiping the dew off our motorcycle in the morning. Although there are "name-brand" hotels along the route, don't be afraid to patronize the smaller, older ones. Just don't expect them to be like the Hilton.

Discounts

If you belong to AAA or CAA, you can get discounts on hotels throughout the U.S. and certain attractions such as the Great Lakes Shipwreck Museum in Whitefish Bay, Michigan. The U.P. Biker Cruising Card is another handy money-saving device. For $10, you can obtain a discount card that's good at restaurants, hotels and bars throughout Michigan's Upper Peninsula. The card never expires and the list of participating businesses continues to grow. If you ride Alger Co. H-58, you can get a patch for your jacket from the website. To acquire a card or a patch, visit **www.upcruising.com**.

Maps

The maps in this book are not intended to be used as navigation aids. I've put them in to give you an idea of the routes we took and the mileage we put in each day. We don't have GPS on our bike, so I can't tell you if it works along Lake Superior. You may wish to carry state highway maps just in case you need them.

Naming Conventions

State highways in Michigan are usually designated as "M-28." However, to avoid confusion with state highways in Minnesota, I refer to Michigan roads as "MI-28" and Minnesota roads as "MN-61."

About Our Bike

Our motorcycle is a 1508cc 2002 Victory Deluxe Touring Cruiser. It has been outfitted with twin dual ceramic coated pipes for better performance and gas mileage. The bike had just 3,000 miles on it when we purchased it in 2007. We've ridden it all over Minnesota, along Route 66 to the Grand Canyon, up Colorado's Million-Dollar Highway, around Lake Superior and followed the Great River Road from the Mississippi's headwaters in Minnesota to its terminus in downtown New Orleans.

Our 2002 Victory Deluxe Touring Cruiser makes our road trips possible.

Highway 13 to Ashland

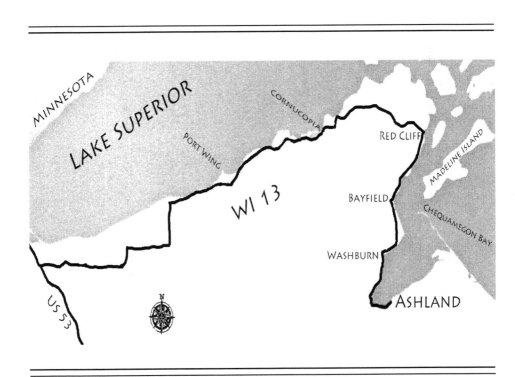

Highway 13 to Ashland

104 Miles

My fifth-grade teacher described Lake Superior as resembling a wolf's head. It's an image that's stuck in my brain throughout my life. If you look at a map, you'll see that the wolf's nose is firmly lodged in the twin ports of Duluth and Superior. Its chin surrounds Chequamegon Bay and extends all the way to Copper Harbor, Michigan. Isle Royale is its slanted eye, and Black Bay and Nipigon Bay in Ontario form its raggedy ear.

Our Lake Superior Circle Tour began east of the tip of the wolf's nose when we hopped off US 53 just past Cutter, Wisconsin, and onto WI-13. With the exception of some dirt roads, 13 is as close as you can get to Lake Superior, and it's the only road that comes close to following the shoreline.

The pavement on this two-lane in northern Wisconsin wasn't brand-new, but it wasn't bad. Within a few miles from where we turned off – in fact, just 11 ½ miles east of Superior -- the road took a decided curve to the north as we crossed the sparkling Amnicon River.

Amnicon is Ojibwe for "where the fish spawn", and the brown river is home to several species of fish, including muskies and brown trout. A sign before the bridge directs you to take Douglas Co. Rd. U to Amnicon Falls State Park. The upper and lower falls at the park are just one of the 42 locations along Lake Superior where you can see water tumble over cliffs and boulders on its way to the lake.

We continued on, skimming over rivers and creeks that snaked and squiggled their way north. Hayfields spread out to our right, shining yellow in the sun. We passed through South Haven, a little place distinguished by a church and a convenience store. The road ran straight before us until we reached a sign for Oulu Glass, where it took 90-degree turn to the north. The pavement was so rough, it even had a permanent sign!

The road wiggled a little, then made another 90-degree curve east. Within minutes, we were traveling through the Brule River Boreal Forest State Natural Area. The path took a hiccup over the Brule, then turned again toward Lake Superior, this time carrying us closer to the lake. We began to smell the cool lake breezes, and then the water came into view

Port Wing soon came into view, too. It's a picturesque little town that hosts a *plein air* painting festival the latter part of July or early August. It's not uncommon to see artists set up along the beach, the harbor or a country road, busily recording what they see in watercolors, acrylic or oils. There's a little park near the western entrance to Port Wing. If you need break, hike back into the woods and visit Twin Falls, a hidden gem.

It's a short drive from Port Wing with hills leading up to Herbster, then Cornucopia. On the way, you'll pass St. Mary's Russian Orthodox Church, a white frame building with the onion domes like the ones you see in pictures of Moscow's Red Square.

"Corny" boasts Wisconsin's northernmost post office.

"Corny" lays claim to the northernmost post office in Wisconsin. When we rode into town, the Tiki Bar at the Village Inn was crowded with bikers. The Village Inn is a B&B, and it has live music in a tent every weekend during the summer. We stayed there once for our wedding anniversary and found the owners friendly and the room quite comfortable.

On our previous visit to Cornucopia, we had tried out Fish Lipps, a local bar and grill next to the post office. Unfortunately, the building had a look of permanent closure about it, so we walked across the street to Ehler's General Store and picked up the makings of a picnic lunch. The 100-year-old store sells organic produce and has a deli. The original owner, Herman Ehlers, is credited with helping local fisherman organize a marketing cooperative so they could compete with larger commercial fisheries.

We drove across the highway to the beach and ate our lunch at the city park on Siskiwit Bay, where we watched a dog frisk in the surf. The sun was bright and the air was clean and beautiful.

The road began calling us, so we hopped aboard the motorcycle and continued on past a series of apple orchards to Red Cliff. The road was rough and we took the downhill ride into Red Cliff at an easy pace.

The Red Cliff reservation is home to the Red Cliff Band of the Lake Superior Chippewa. The reservation is a mile wide and 13 miles long – not a lot of space for 940-some residents. The area still has the run-down look of poverty, although the tribe's financial fortunes have been on the upswing since it opened its Legendary Waters resort and casino in 2012. The tribe, which was formerly completely dependent on commercial fishing, also runs a fish hatchery. The Red Cliff Band holds its annual pow-wow in July. Expect crowds in Red Cliff if you travel at that time.

It's just three miles from Red Cliff to Bayfield, a town that's been a tourist destination since the late 1800s, when the well-heeled from other parts of the country began spending summers in northern Wisconsin. Their huge Victorian summer homes are now historic bed-and-breakfast establishments. On summer and fall weekends, downtown Bayfield looks like the midway at the Minnesota State Fair – wall-to-wall people. Hotels and B&Bs fill up quickly, and restaurants are crowded.

Still, Bayfield has a lot to offer in terms of shopping – you can buy everything from hoodies to local art – and entertainment. You may want to try sea kayaking; there are several sea caves to explore in the area. Bayfield is also where you can catch the ferry to nearby Madeline Island, the largest island in the Apostle Islands group.

Highway 13 continues to follow the outline of Chequamagon Bay, passing through little places such as Salmo and Sioux before it reaches the city of Washburn, named after one of Wisconsin's governors. Its quaint downtown is decidedly less busy than Bayfield's.

It was getting close to five o'clock and we had left Minneapolis at six in the morning. We came to a roundabout at the junction of Hwy. 13 and US2. It spun us gently in the direction of Ashland, where we were glad to pull into our hotel. We had rounded the wolf's lower lip.

Madeline Island

Treat yourself (and your bike) to a ride on the Madeline Island Ferry.

Madeline Island

34-mile loop

Madeline Island isn't on everyone's version of the Lake Superior Circle Tour, but it should be. A ride around the largest of the 22 Apostle Islands is fun, and you can treat your bike to a ferry ride from Bayfield.

Ferry service between Bayfield and La Pointe, the only town on the only occupied island in the Apostle group, began in the 1860s. Ferry service is offered daily throughout the year; even when Superior freezes over in the winter, one of the ferries has enough horsepower to plow through eight inches of ice! When the ice is too thick for the ferry to handle, islanders build an ice road and drive their vehicles across the lake.

In the summer, the double-ended ferries cross the 2.6-mile channel every forty-five minutes. As the tourist season winds down, the trips become less frequent. At the time of this writing, the fare for a motorcycle and two adults is $42 round-trip.

The line to board the ferry was long, so I dismounted and bought the tickets while Ralph maneuvered the Victory into the queue. The crew knew just exactly where to park every vehicle. They reserved a special place for motorcycles under the ferry's upper deck next to the bridge. As I walked onto the ferry, I heard the captain say, "I've got a plan. If this ferry sinks, rip the covers off the boats and jump in." It earned him a few chuckles.

It takes about twenty minutes to cross from the mainland to Madeline Island. It's great to be on the lake, watching the water slide by. Looking aft, you see the hillsides of Bayfield recede but never disappear from view. Looking forward, you see the landing at La Pointe, with sailboats bobbing in the marina.

After the ferry docked and was securely tied to the wharf, the captain let down the gangplank and Ralph started the Victory. Within minutes, we took a right and began rolling down La Pointe's exceedingly crowded Main Street. Like Bayfield, it's a popular summer vacation destination (the town's population expands from 302 in winter to 1,500).

We took another right at the Old Fort Rd. and headed toward the island's south shore, passing the Robert Trent Jones-designed golf course. Barely one block away from the ferry landing, if you take another right on Chief Buffalo Lane, you'll come to the old Ojibwe cemetery. Some of the graves date back to 1836, and many are covered with little wooden spirit houses where the Ojibwe left food and offerings to help the deceased enter the spirit world. It's a sacred site to the Ojibwe – they consider the entire island as their homeland.

The Old Fort Rd. refers to a fort that was built on the southwestern tip of the island in 1692 by Chevalier Pierre Le Seuer. The American Fur Company moved the fort to the present-day site of La Pointe about 1832.

As we neared the southeastern tip of the island, we took a left from the Old Fort Rd. onto South Shore Drive. Although the top speed anywhere on Madeline is 40 mph, it's a beautiful coastal drive, and one not to be rushed. Superior's cold blue waters sparkled in the summer sun. The air was brisk and the dark green pines provided an elegant backdrop. We followed the road all the way to the entrance to Big Bay State Park, then doubled back. The park has a wonderful beach, but we were there for the ride.

We drove back the way we came and took a right on Co. Rd. H, also known as Black Shanty Rd. After a mile, the road took a sharp angle to the right and became Big Bay Rd. It curved through the woods, then the lake reappeared at our side.

As we neared northeastern end of Madeline Island, the road came to a T and we turned left onto Schoolhouse Rd. We crossed the island's three-mile width in no time at all and found ourselves cruising along the North Shore Rd. We caught glimpses of large estates tucked into the woods. Like Bayfield in the nineteenth century, Madeline has become the summer haven of the well-to-do. As we cruised westward down the island's 14-mile length, the road took us closer to the shore.

Coming closer to town, we stopped to take a look at the Madeline Island airport. This small, two-runway airport doesn't even have a control tower, but it handles 116 planes per day during the summer. Its significance to me and Ralph is deeper, however, because in 1978, somewhere along the road from the airport to the ferry, Cupid's arrow hit its mark.

It was early spring. We had flown with his parents in a small rented plane for a Sunday afternoon in Bayfield. Ralph's father, Joe, was the pilot and Ralph took the second chair. His mother Arlene and I sat in the back. Joe landed the plane smoothly on the runway and we walked the two miles to the ferry landing. The tourist season hadn't begun yet, but the ferry was operating. A few shops were open, and we poked through those. We admired the fine Victorian homes.

We decided to have a snack before re-boarding the ferry for the ride back to Madeline. Most restaurants were not open. The one that was quickly ran out of food because of the unexpected crush of visitors. Ralph asked for a root beer float – it was served with chocolate ice cream. Joe settled for pistachio pie. It was the most brilliant shade of green I've ever seen. As we walked back to the airport, lagging behind his parents, Ralph and I both knew it had been a life-changing day. In another 18 months, we were married.

Madeline Island has changed greatly since then. We could see the changes as we rode into town along Big Bay Blvd. There are more –and fancier – places to stay. There are more shops and places to eat. But it's still a great ride.

Ashland to Copper Harbor

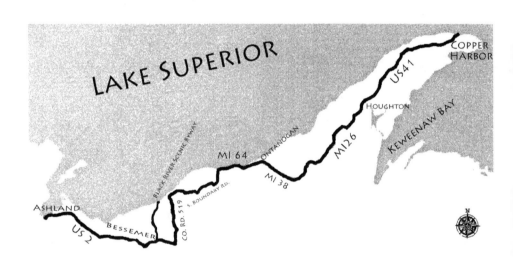

Ashland to Copper Harbor

197 miles

It was clear, sunny and crisp when we left Ashland and headed east on US 2 toward Michigan. I had a hoodie on underneath my leathers and it felt good.

US 2 runs straight through downtown Ashland past the Xcel Energy plant, car dealerships and manufacturing plants. It stays pretty close to the shoreline. Past Ashland, it takes a 45-degree angle and makes a beeline through the Bad River Indian Reservation. Smooth and straight, it's a no-nonsense drive, almost as though the Wisconsin Department of Transportation wants you to get through Indian County as soon as possible.

It's also a heavily wooded area. Tall trees line both sides of the road. The highway skims through little places such as Odanah, Birch, Cedar and Saxon. The Bad River Casino lies midway between Odanah and Birch. Its red exterior comes as a surprise after traveling through the forest. The parking lot was full, despite its remote location. A little while later, we crossed the Wisconsin-Michigan state line just northwest of Ironwood.

At Bessemer, a large fiberglass statue of a skier advertising Big Powderhorn Mountain prompted us to make a U-turn and do a little sight-seeing. We turned right on Monroe Street and headed north. In a few blocks, the road was re-named Black River Road.

The road loosely followed the twists and turns of the Black River as it flowed toward Lake Superior. We passed Copper Peak, which boasts the world's largest artificial ski slide. For $20, you can ride the chairlift and then take an 18-story elevator to the top of an observation tower and look out over three states and Canada. We declined that opportunity and continued to ride along Black River Road, also known as Gogebic Co. 513.

The road is also a National Scenic Byway. There are five waterfalls along the 14-mile route: Great Conglomerate Falls, Potawatomi, Gorge, Sandstone, and Rainbow Falls. We chose to get off and visit Potawatomi and Gorge Falls. The same parking area serves both cataracts. There is an eighth of a mile between them.

The falls are not far from the road. The trails to them are a series of wooden steps and balconies. As we paused and looked at the falls through a frame of hemlock branches, it was easy to see how the Black River got its name. As it winds through the shadows, the water does indeed look black – until it tumbles and boils over boulders. Gorge Falls has a 34-foot drop. The sound of rushing water can just about drown a conversation.

After we had looked our fill, we made a pit stop at the restroom near the parking lot, then continued down the road. It ended at a marina on Lake Superior, the only harbor and marina operated by the U.S. Forest Service in the continental U.S.

We turned back toward Bessemer. As we ascended a hill, a doe and her fawn crossed the road in front of us. Ralph slowed almost to a halt as the fawn followed uncertainly after its mother.

We looked at a map and decided the "official" Lake Superior circle route would take us too far from the lake. We had heard that Gogebic Co. 519 was a good motorcycle route, so we decided to try it out. We drove back through Bessemer on US 2 and made a left turn at Co. 519 in Wakefield, passing through the town and by Sunday Lake, which looked very inviting.

As we traversed the twisting two-lane road, we had our second wildlife encounter of the day. A large dark bird suddenly rose up from the pavement. It was a heavy bird and it struggled to get to get airborne as we bore down upon it. I sat behind Ralph and chanted, "Go, bird, go!" and I knew Ralph was thinking the same thing. He revved the throttle and the bird continued to fly ever-so-slowly ahead of us. Just as it looked as if we were going to end up with a very large feathered passenger on the fairing, the bird caught enough lift. I leaned back and snapped a photo as we zoomed beneath it. It's a blurry photo, but the ugly, bald red head of a turkey vulture is unmistakable.

Co. 519 is a good motorcycle road, but it's not without its challenges. There were several low spots and patches of sand, gravel and stone, and it was bumpy. Ralph couldn't decide to run through the middle of the lane or drive in the car tracks – it didn't seem to make a difference.

Co. 519 blended into the Boundary Road and the riding got curvier. It was also bumpy. We came upon some mysterious white patches in the road that made the Victory's rear tire bump from side to side. We continued to wind our way north. Suddenly, Lake Superior was right in front of us. We could go only left or right.

End of the road....

Porcupine Mountain State Park was on our left, but we were headed east. We made a right turn onto the 107th Engineers Memorial Highway. We were astonished to see what looked like a fairly decent motel just east of where the Union River empties into Superior. It was completely abandoned. What made this so remarkable was that the beach – and the lake – were right across the road! It was one of many abandoned properties we saw in the Upper Peninsula, and a good reminder that beautiful scenery doesn't always provide a good living.

Past Silver City, once a ghost town but now boasting 15 businesses, the Engineers Hwy. morphed into MI-64. It hugged the shore until we reached

Ontanogan. We took a brief dip southeast on MI-38, then grabbed MI-26 to ride up the middle of the Keweenaw Peninsula.

It's a beautiful ride, surrounded by tall pines. The scenery is broken, now and again, by small cabins and odd signs. Near the town of Toivala, there was a sign proclaiming "deer head boiling," followed by a phone number. Apparently there's a guy tucked into the woods up there, ready to turn your prized buck into a bleached skeleton to mount over your cabin door.

We saw little traffic until we reached Houghton, home of Michigan Technical University. As we turned to cross the bridge over the Houghton Canal into neighboring Hancock, I glimpsed a sign: "No snowmobiles on sidewalks." Houghton must be a fun place in the winter!

After crossing the bridge, MI-26 snakes off to the right. We turned left on US 41. It winds through Hancock, and slowly climbs past stately old mansions and out of town past the Quincy Mine. Out in the country again, we passed through old copper-mining towns in quick succession: Calumet, Kearsarge (named after a Civil War battleship, but featuring

a stone ship that looks like a World War II destroyer), Allouez (home of left-handed baseball pitcher George Brunet who became a Mexican league hall of famer), Ahmeek (Ojibwe for "beaver"), and Mohawk.

Four miles north of Mohawk is a 32-ft.-tall snow gauge. Keeping track of snow depth is a big deal on the Upper Peninsula, where snowmobiles are often the winter vehicle of choice (or necessity). The highest amount recorded at the top of the snow gauge is 390.4 inches during the winter of 1978-79. The previous year's snowfall is marked by an arrow that slides up and down the gauge.

When the snow gets this deep in the Upper Peninsula, it's too late to head south!

Fortunately, no snow fell in August. After tracing curve after curve along MI-26, we came to Copper Harbor.

Copper Harbor is a throwback to the early to mid-1960s. Marriott and Holiday Inn have made no inroads here. The motels are of the mom-and-pop variety. There are no chain restaurants. Life moves at a slower pace here, marked by the seasons.

We had booked into the King Copper Motel and were rewarded with a lakeside room. The pink bathroom tile was straight out of the '50s, but the room was clean. We unloaded our gear, put on our tennis shoes and walked over to the Mariner North for supper.

Sunset at Copper Harbor

We sat down at the bar and Ralph asked the bartender what he had on tap. "I suppose you'll want me to recite the whole damn list and then you'll choose Miller Lite," was the slightly grumpy reply. Ralph then asked about local brews. The bartender cheered up a little then and became more sociable. I asked about the pronunciation of "Keweenaw" (CUE-ee-naw, an Indian word for "portage"), and ordered a whitefish sandwich.

Gradually, we shed the road miles as we relaxed and compared notes on the day's ride. We set out to walk the town until sunset. I snapped a few photos on my cell phone and tried to send them back home, but there was no cell service.

It's Christmas year-round in Christmas, Michigan.

A Town Called Christmas

It sounded cute: Christmas, Michigan. For me, it also sounded like the perfect shopping opportunity, and a chance to get in out of the rain. It was only four and a half miles west of Munising.

As we entered the town, we came up on a faded, weather-beaten green wooden sign with bullet holes in it. The sign bore a likeness of Santa Claus, and the greeting, "Welcome to Christmas." We pulled off of M-28 and into the parking lot of Santa's Workshop gift shop, where a 35-ft.-tall plywood Santa waved us in.

We received a warm welcome from the gift shop owner, Sharon Tesch, who looked as though she would have welcomed anyone on that gray, rainy day, including a couple of soggy bikers. The store was warm and cozy and decorated Christmas trees lined the aisles. It truly is Christmas all year-round in the workshop: Santa holds court every Sunday from 2 p.m. to close March through November. In December, he shifts into overdrive and makes appearances on Saturdays as well.

Although Tesch had lovely Royal Copenhagen, Pipka and Christopher Radko ornaments, I was delighted to find some locally-made treasures. They were cut from wood and had decoupaged designs of Mary, Joseph and Jesus on them. They had a Russian Orthodox look, and they were signed on the back by "Santa Jim". Best of all, they were perfectly flat, could slip neatly into the Victory's saddlebags and wouldn't break.

As we waited while Sharon rang up my purchase, I asked her how Christmas got its name. It seems that a man named Julius Thorson built a toy factory in the area in 1938 and called it "Christmas." In June 1940, the factory burned to the ground. It's not known whether he was disheartened or simply didn't have the money to rebuild, but Thorson left town. Even though he moved on, the Christmas name stuck.

About 400 people live in Christmas. Many of them are involved in tourism, which has struggled mightily throughout the Upper Peninsula for many years. The town seems a little worn. There are a number of small, Christmas-y places to stay, including the Christmas Motel, Evergreen Cottage, White Pine Lodge and Yule Log Resort. You can even stay in a yurt at the Paddlers Village on Scrooge's Alley. Relatively new on the scene is the Kewadin Casino, owned and operated by the Sault tribe of the Chippewa. It doesn't have lodging space in Christmas, but it does offer Frosty's Bar and Grille.

As we mounted up, I took a last look at the red-and-green exterior of Santa's Workshop. I hope Christmas lasts forever.

Copper Harbor to Munising

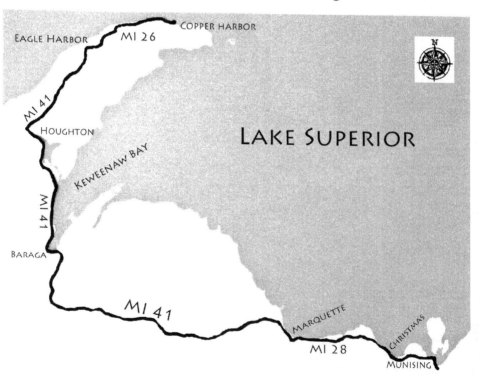

Copper Harbor to Munising

189 miles

It was overcast in the morning. Ralph predicted that the rain we had experienced in Minneapolis before leaving home would soon catch up to us.

We strolled through downtown Copper Harbor to the Tamarack Inn for breakfast. The restaurant has a few sleeping rooms attached to it. As we entered the restaurant, a Floridian bundled up in a heavy sweatshirt complained that he hadn't been able get any heat in his

MI-26 to Eagle Harbor

room the previous night. "It's cold here!" he exclaimed. We laughed and told him he had just experienced "good sleeping weather."

As the waitress brought our coffee, I had a chance to ask about some berries I had seen on our walk the previous evening. One looked like a flat-topped red raspberry, the other a blueberry. Unlike wild blueberries, however, the plant grew tall and the berries were actually out of my reach. She said the red berry was a thimbleberry and the blue one was a bilberry. Thimbleberries are too delicate for commercial use, but folks in the Keweenaw Peninsula make excellent jam out of them. Similarly, bilberries are considered too small for commercial use, but local shops carry homemade bilberry jam. The waitress asked where we saw them. I had a hunch she was going berry-picking in the near future.

We walked back to the bike, put the kickstand up and rode west out of Copper Harbor on MI-26, intending to tour the lighthouse at Eagle Harbor. Unfortunately, we're early risers and the lighthouse doesn't open until 10 a.m. We walked around the light and looked out at Lake Superior, then took to the road once more. Below Eagle Harbor, MI-26 became MI-41, and we rode on to Hancock, where we stopped to take a look at the old Quincy Mine.

Copper has been mined in the Keweenaw Peninsula for more than 7,000 years. Early European explorers were greatly excited to find Native Americans wearing copper jewelry and using copper tools. The Quincy Mine was a major producer of copper ore from 1846 to 1945. In that time, it produced 1.5 billion lbs. of copper and paid more than $30 million in dividends to its investors. It paid dividends so regularly that people called it "Old Reliable." The company continued to produce copper from waste ore until 1967, when it finally closed down.

Today the Quincy Mine is part of the Keweenaw National Historical Park. You can take a tour of the above-ground portions of the mine for $12. You can also take a cog-rail tramcar tour down to the seventh level of the mine. The full tour is $20. If you are a AAA member, you can get discounted admission. We wandered around the grounds and looked at the old, rusting mining equipment, including a steam engine, mineral cars and a drill. A mist began to fall, and we decided it was time to move. We took the time to put on our rain suits, and I was glad we did.

We crossed the bridge back into Houghton. The rain came down heavier and harder as we followed the highway around the tip of Keweenaw Bay at Baraga and on through Marquette, the largest city in the U.P. I thought I must look like some kind of alien being with my pink-

The Quincy Mine was once known as "Old Reliable."

and-gray rain suit and my Captain America stars-and-stripes motorcycle helmet – a real lunar fashion faux pas --, but the suit did an excellent job of keeping out both water and wind.

We stopped in the town of Christmas for a little shopping, then pushed on to Munising. The sky was a sodden mass of lumpy gray clouds. The lake was a choppy sheet of lead.

We stopped for lunch at Muldoon's Pasties. Headquartered in a bright yellow frame house on M-28, the restaurant was a beacon of warmth. The rich, onion-y smell of fresh-baked pasties beckoned like a cartoon finger as we approached.

Inside, we placed our orders (Original Beef for Ralph, chicken for me). The front of the house was crowded with souvenirs ranging from T-shirts proclaiming Muldoon's Pasties as "U.P. Soul Food" to a "Yooperland" Border Patrol hat and homemade fudge. There weren't many places to sit (it is, after all, a house), and the drizzle had let up, so we gathered up some ketchup packets and took our steaming sandwiches outside to a picnic table.

After a long, wet morning on a motorcycle, poking a plastic fork into a fresh pasty was pure delight. The savory smells of potatoes, onions, rutabagas, meat and fresh bread combined into a true comfort food experience. Fortified by the food that sustained the area's copper miners, we got back on our Victory and headed east on M-28.

***

Pasties

Here's a recipe for pasties that I picked up at the Quincy Mine. Unless you're feeding a crew of miners, you probably won't want to make the entire recipe. I cut it in half when I made them at home.

3 lbs. potatoes, diced

1 cup carrots, diced

2 cups onions, diced

2 cups rutabaga, diced

2 lbs. ground meat or diced fish

Season to taste

Take about a dozen 4-oz. pie crust dough balls that have been cooled then warmed to room temperature. Roll each into a 10-inch oval. Put 10 oz. of pasty filling on one side of a dough sheet, pull the rest over the top and crimp the edge. Bake for 1 hour at 350 degrees.

Alger County H-8

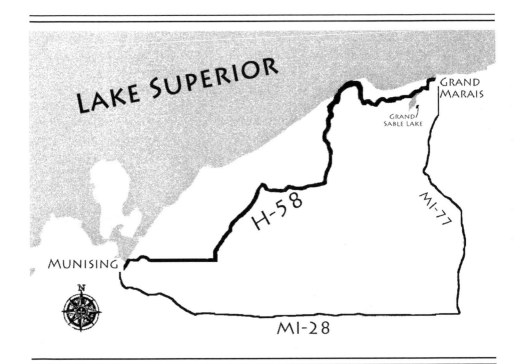

Alger County H-58

69 miles

We first learned about H-58 when we began planning our Lake Superior tour. There wasn't a lot of information about the highway in the Upper Peninsula guidebook I had picked up at a motorcycle show, except that it had been paved recently and contained 198 curves. "We gotta ride this," I told Ralph.

Near the U.S. Forest Ranger Station in Munising, M-28 hooks off to the south. We continued straight onto East Munising Avenue and H-58, past the Neenah paper mill and across the Anna River. Lake Superior's cold waters licked the shoreline on our left as we crossed Tannery Creek. H-58 began to bend away from the lake and we were soon surrounded by the Hiawatha National Forest.

This section of the county highway is also known as the Adams Trail, and it's pretty much a straight shot from the Pictured Rocks Golf Club, cutting through a swampy lake to just shortly after Shingleton Road, where it begins to curve to the northeast. It's such a straight shot that I began to wonder where those 198 curves were. I needn't have worried. H-58 does not disappoint.

The pavement is smooth and shows little signs of wear and tear. Although parts of the road have existed since the 1920s, H-58 was not fully paved until 2010. The paving caused a ruckus among local residents, who protested the action loudly. At one point, the protest got downright nasty: Nails were strewn across the highway; no one stepped forward to claim responsibility.

Homes and farms hide in the woods along the highway. We rode H-58 on an August Monday and had it all to ourselves, every last curve.

The blacktop began to snake through the woods like a black velvet ribbon, bringing us past empty stretches where forest fires had cleared the area. The curves and twisties came in bunches as we raced along. The double yellow lines dividing the highway blurred. Roads sneaked off into the woods beside us, but we clung to H-58, intent on the ride.

We crossed streams and squiggled our way between lakes. Curve after curve, we drove closer to Lake Superior, far closer than you can ever get on the "official" Circle Route. I caught occasional glimpses of water through the trees, and the fresh scent of the lake was in the air.

We crossed the Hurricane River (H-58 is also known as the "Hurricane Highway"), and swooped by the entrance to the Pictured Rocks National Lakeshore. By this time, we were so caught up in the ride that stopping was unthinkable. The highway turns to the southeast and becomes known as the Au Sable Trail. If you follow the road to the Log Slide, you can hike down a path to see the Au Sable Lighthouse and the Grand Sable Dunes.

Somewhere in this area, we came across a sign that said, "Hills and curves, next 3.5 miles." I had just enough time to wonder, "What the hell have we been doing?" when the country become hillier and the curves tighter and more numerous. Ralph didn't have much time to shift gears as we leaned right and left over and over again.

We twisted along the northern edges of Grand Sable Lake before H-58 suddenly became tame just east of the entrance to the Grand Sable Visitor Center. It made a 90-degree turn to the north at the intersection with Co. Rd. 770, then made a sweeping curve to the east where Sable Falls Road connects. A long, sweeping S curve brought us into Grand Marais and deposited us at the shore of Lake Superior. With a population of about 300, it's about one-fourth the sizes of Grand Marais, Minnesota.

H-58 crosses Grand Marais Ave. and moseys along the shoreline for a little while before the pavement abruptly gives way to gravel. The section from Grand Marais to Deer Park was still gravel when we traveled through the area, and we decided to skip it.

Time to head back to the Circle Route.

After you've ridden H-58, you can get a patch at **www.upcruising.com**.

Alger County H-58 offers 198 curves in 69 miles.

Grand Marais to Paradise

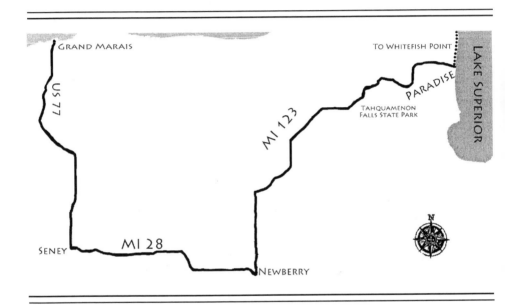

Grand Marais to Paradise

115 miles

Grand Marais, Michigan, is far different from Grand Marais, Minnesota.

The town on the Upper Peninsula was first visited by French explorers Radisson and Grossilliers in 1660. Although "grand marais" translates as "big marsh," Walter Romig, author of *Michigan Place Names*, asserts that in the French used by the voyageurs, it meant a small harbor. Permanent settlement in the area began just after the Civil War. Commercial fishing was the basis for its economy. Today, the Michigan town is a tourist destination.

The town on Minnesota's North Shore also received its name during the days of the fur trade. Settlement there didn't really get started until the 1870s. Iron ore, lumber and fishing were the economic drivers. Grand Marais, Minnesota, has evolved away from its roots to become not only a tourist destination, but an arts colony as well. It's also four times the size of its Michigan counterpart.

Although it would have been nice to spend some time poking around in Grand Marais, the day was getting on and our destination, Paradise, was still a good ways away. Unfortunately, there were no paved roads to take us on a direct line from Grand Marais to Paradise, so we headed south on US 77 and re-joined the "official" circle route. It felt as though we were a long way away from Lake Superior.

The rain had ended during our ride on H-58. Although the sun didn't poke its head out from the clouds, the day seemed brighter. We made a left turn onto MI-28 at Seney and took aim at Newberry. The roads had some curves but were generally unremarkable.

We caught MI-123 at Newberry. The highway started out

arrow-straight, then began to zigzag. By the time we reached Tahquamenon Falls State Park, it had begun to curve with regularity. We noted the location of the park and kept on. Paradise was within reach!

In a matter of minutes, we rode into the parking lot at Curley's Motel. It's a distinctly '60s motel, with the typical neon signage of that era. One sign proudly proclaims "Color TV". Another warns that the beach in front of the property is for guests only. Others will be charged $10 to visit. How they enforce that rule, I don't know.

Owner Linda Ferguson greeted us and provided a rag to wipe off the motorcycle in the morning. The motel room was small by today's standards. The queen-sized bed filled most of it and the bathroom was about two feet wide. The room was clean and had a view of Lake Superior, and we were satisfied. Unfortunately, the drizzle began again, so we couldn't sit out on the beach and watch the waves roll in.

We ate bison burgers at the Yukon Inn across the road from Curley's. Although it had great log cabin atmosphere, the food was not that great. The restaurant has since closed.

The following morning we headed to the Berry Patch Bakery for breakfast, then down 123 to Tahquamenon Falls State Park. We followed another motorcyclist down a curvy road to the park entrance. A motorcycle permit to enter the park cost $8.40 at the time of our visit.

There are several waterfalls in the park. The highest is the Upper Falls, which is 200 feet wide and cascades over a 50-ft. precipice. A wooden staircase takes you to the Lower Falls; I counted 96 steps. The lower falls – there are five altogether – are a series of falls that tumble around an island. We rented a rowboat for $6 per person and rowed as close to them as we could. Tahquamenon gets its name from the Ojibwe word for "dark water," and it lives up to its name.

After our Tahquamenon tour, we rode back to Paradise, turned left and headed north up to the lighthouse at Whitefish Point. The retired light station is the home of the Great Lakes Shipwreck Museum. The numbers are in dispute, but there are 550 known shipwrecks in Lake Superior. The first was the Invincible in 1816. The most famous may be the Edmund Fitzgerald, which disappeared off of Whitefish Point in 1975.

Gordon Lightfoot's "Wreck of the Edmund Fitzgerald" was playing as

Upper Tahquamenon Falls is worth a side trip.

we entered the museum. I gave an inward groan, thinking that we might have to listen to the saga (which I love, just not continuously) throughout our visit. That would have been maudlin. But just as there are other shipwrecks, there are other shipwreck songs, and the museum plays them, too.

Although it has the Fitz's great brass bell, the museum takes great pains to present information about other wrecks. The museum grounds also includes the lighthouse and the Crews Quarters, where you can stay overnight and get a personalized tour of the light and the museum for $150 per night, double occupancy. Admission to the museum is $13 per adult, and there is an AAA discount.

We spent an hour or more looking at exhibits, the light and the lakeshore, then mounted up again. Canada was calling.

Paradise to Batchawana

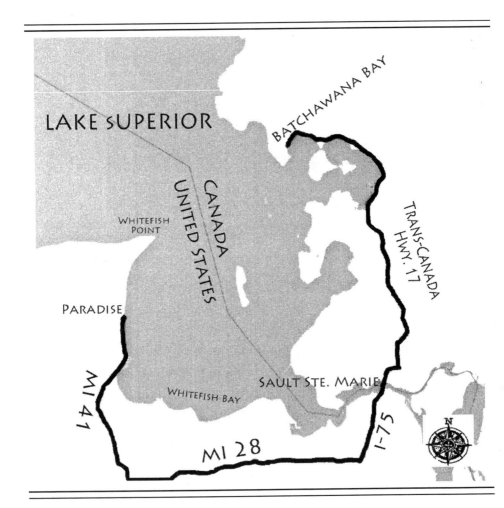

LAKE SUPERIOR

BATCHAWANA BAY

WHITEFISH
POINT

CANADA
UNITED STATES

TRANS-CANADA
HWY. 17

PARADISE

MI 41

WHITEFISH BAY

SAULT STE. MARIE

MI 28

I-75

N

Entry into Canada

107 miles

The guard at the border crossing was suspicious. We had just handed our U.S. passports over to him, and he scrutinized them carefully. "Why were you in Amsterdam, Mr. Sowden?"

"I was there on a business trip."

"What kind of business? What do you do for a living?"

"I'm an electrical engineer."

"What is your purpose for coming to Canada?"

"Vacation. To ride around Lake Superior."

Satisfied at last, the guard waved us through. There's no more free passage between the U.S. and Canada. There hasn't been since the Twin Towers were destroyed in a terrorist attack in New York in 2001. Even the best of neighbors can't be too careful these days.

It was a quick trip south from Paradise on US 41 to MI-28, then up I-75 to the international bridge at Sault Ste. Marie. There's a toll plaza just before you reach the bridge. We paid a $3 fee (check www.saultbridge.com for current rates and wait times) and joined the line to cross the bridge. It was rush hour, and many Canadians were returning home from work in the U.S.

Sault Ste. Marie, Ontario, welcomes you in two languages.

Construction of the bridge started in 1960. At this writing, it is undergoing some upgrades, including LED lights across the span.

It was exhilarating to look down at the Soo Locks 124 feet below us as we drove the nearly three-mile span. After our encounter at the Canadian border station, we began a slow drive through Sault Ste. Marie, Ontario.

Sault Ste. Marie dates back to 1668, when Father Jacques Marquette (who has his name all over the Midwest), established a mission at the rapids that connect Lake Superior with Lake Huron. He named it Sainte Marie du Sault; *sault* (soo) is French for rapids. It was strategically placed and quickly became the center of the North American fur trade. A canal was built after Michigan became a state in 1836, and the area later became a place of passage for ships carrying iron ore from Minnesota to the steel plants in Pennsylvania. Sault Ste. Marie, Ontario, is about twice the size of Sault Ste. Marie, Michigan, but the United States government controls the locks on the St. Mary's River that separates the two.

The neighborhood immediately north of the international bridge is in an older part of town. We followed the signs directing us to the Trans-Canada Highway, making a right turn onto Huron St., then another right onto Queen St., which brought us under the bridge we had just crossed and onto Cameron's Way. I glimpsed many brick homes as we wound our way through the edge of the city. I recall seeing a neon-green house in one neighborhood that screamed, "Look at me!"

Cameron's Way came to a T at Second Line Ave., also known as Ontario 550. At the Great Northern Rd., we turned left and began our journey on the Trans-Canada. We were immediately welcomed by a Wal-Mart, Home Depot and Best Buy and felt as if we'd never left home. Fortunately, we were soon out of town.

The sun was shining when we left Michigan and the U.S. behind. As we hit the open road outside of Sault St. Marie, a light fog rolled in from the lake. The drizzle that had dogged us for much of the previous day caught up to us again.

Trans-Canada Hwy. 17 is one arm of the highway system that connects all ten Canadian provinces. The stretch around Lake Superior is beautifully maintained. It moves inland from Sault Ste. Marie, then starts heading shoreward near Hayden. We crossed the Goulais River. The road began to

The drive into Lake Shore Resort in Batchawana Bay.

move ever closer to the shore and began hugging it at Havilland. Rocky outcroppings lined one side of the road, while Superior's waters gently lapped the other. The curves were easy.

Our destination for the evening was Batchawana Bay, which is the midpoint for the entire Trans-Canada system. "Batchawana" is an Ojibwe word meaning, "water bubbles up." A strong current between Batchawana Island and Sand Point causes this bubbling action. The Hudson Bay Company once maintained a trading post where the Batchawana River drains into the lake, and the Ojibwe had spirit houses like the ones on Madeline Island up in the hills behind the lake.

We had booked a room at the Lake Shore Resort, which advertises lake views and bedsheets dried in the sun. Its Salzburger Hof restaurant serves genuine Austrian cuisine and has been featured in "Where to Eat in Canada" for more than 25 years. The owners, the Elsigan family, are very welcoming of motorcyclists. It sounded marvelous and it was.

Signs pointed the way from the highway to the resort. It was a long, slow, 3 km drive down a wet dirt road. We passed a white church with black trim and a copper steeple. Seagulls lined its roof from front to back. In a little while, we came to the resort. A stately double row of conically-shaped yews lined the gravel driveway, which was marked by American and Canadian flags.

We were shown to our room, which was large enough to be a lake cabin. I could have set up housekeeping if it had had a kitchen! In addition to a sitting area overlooking the lake, the room had a porch with a table for playing games. We were feeling hungry, however, and strolled over to the Salzburger Hof, a building decorated with German-style *fachwerk* on the outside.

We were somewhat surprised when we were asked if we had reservations. "No…but we're staying here tonight." The restaurant is apparently where locals about the age of our parents hang out on Friday night. For them, it's like an old country club, where the host knows everyone's name, what they usually order and what they drink.

Despite our lack of credentials, we were seated and we ordered drinks. The menus came and they were was full of Austrian and German goodies. I went for the Hungarian goulash with spaetzle. It was delicious, but the plate that came to the table could easily have satisfied three people.

An after-dinner walk to the lake became a necessity. We lumbered down the hill to the shore, where a campfire grate sat in the sand. Ralph began skipping rocks into the lake. I found some thimbleberries and, even though I felt as though I couldn't eat one thing more, I put one in my mouth. It was sweeter than a raspberry and juicy.

Low gray clouds scudded over us and the western horizon took on a slightly pink hue. Perhaps tomorrow would be a sunnier day.

Watch out for logging trucks!

Batchawana to Nipigon

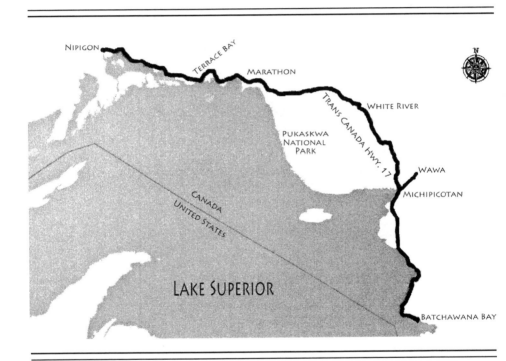

NIPIGON

TERRACE BAY

MARATHON

WHITE RIVER

TRANS CANADA HWY. 17

PUKASKWA
NATIONAL
PARK

WAWA

MICHIPICOTAN

CANADA
UNITED STATES

LAKE SUPERIOR

BATCHAWANA BAY

Batchawana to Nipigon

521 miles

We didn't necessarily want to ride around the back of the wolf's head and up to the tip of his ear in one day, but across the Trans-Canada Highway, there was no room at the inn. It was a long, but beautiful, ride.

The weather was gray and foggy when we left Batchawana Bay, but the sun soon burned through the clouds and mist. We stopped at Agawa Crafts and the Canadian Carver in Pancake Bay to top off the Victory's gas tank. Just a few miles north of Batchawana, Pancake Bay supposedly got its name during the fur-trading days when voyageurs who were running short of supplies would stop for a quick meal of pancakes before heading into Sault Ste. Marie.

The stores' porches were filled with wonderful woodcarvings and native crafts. We wandered inside to see more. It was a strange blend of tourist-y items and high-end wood carvings. Some of the carvings in the Canadian Carver seemed to flow organically from the logs from which they were sculpted. Fish and eagles, wolves and people were rendered with exquisite skill. I envied the carvers' ability to "see" images in the wood. Unfortunately, the pieces I enjoyed most were either out of budget or too large to carry on the bike. Native-made items ran the gamut from arrow quivers made of coyote to mukluks made of moose or deer hide.

Realizing we had a long way to go, we climbed aboard the Victory again and continued along the lake shore. Rocky cliffs guarded the road, which was beautifully paved and well marked.

We crossed the Montreal River and entered the Lake Superior Provincial Park, where we encountered more fog and rain. The road wound through the park and we stopped for a quick lunch before continuing north. We ignored the signs pointing to Wawa and continued on Hwy. 17, which is curvier than the road maps suggest.

The Michipicoten First Nations Reserve was on our left as the road began to make a wide arc not only around the reservation but Pukaskwa National Park as well. There are roads leading to the park, but they're all gravel. I envied the people of the First Nation: They have that corner of Lake Superior all to themselves.

It was in this wilderness setting that I began seeing little human-shaped rock formations on the hillsides along the road. They seemed to be deliberately placed.

We came to a bright orange sign in the middle of absolutely nowhere. The graphic looked the bottom set of teeth on a Halloween jack o'lantern. We soon learned that this meant "rough road." Really rough road!

Winnie the Pooh is honored at a park in White River, Ontario.

We stopped for gas in White River, which was where Winnie the Pooh was born. Winnie was actually a little black bear cub that had been found by a trapper and brought to town to be sold as a pet. (The White River website says bears were common pets in the early 1900s.) The trapper sold the bear to Lt. Harry Coleburn, who was training to fight in World War I.

Coleburn, who was born in England, claimed Winnipeg, Manitoba, as his home town. He named the bear "Winnie" and took her to England with him, where she slept under his cot in a tent on Salisbury Plain. When he was called to fight in France, she was placed in the London Zoo. Winnie became a favorite of many zoo goers, including A.A. Milne and his son, Christopher. Milne later made Winnie the star of his children's books. In 1992, White River dedicated a statue of Winnie the Pooh, which stands in a park along Hwy. 17.

While we were at the gas station in White River, I lost the post from my chaps buckle. Without it, I couldn't keep my chaps on. I dug through the saddle bags to find something – anything – to hold them up. The carabiner clip from my steel water bottle seemed like a good solution. I clipped the two sides of the belt together. It was awkward, and it probably looked stupid, but it worked.

We drove on, getting deeper into the Canadian wilderness. I've heard many bikers say that there's "nothing" in Canada. While I'll admit that the towns along the Trans-Canada are few and far between, and there's nothing resembling the kind of nightlife you might find in Chicago or New York, there is still plenty to see.

Relax and enjoy Ontario's scenery.

Cliffs rise alongside the highway, presenting a slightly red, rocky face to the world. Enchanting fairy-tale islands float in lakes that shimmer in the sun. One can almost see a castle – or a cabin – hidden amongst the dark pines. Hillsides of pine undulate across the horizon and rivers tumble under the highway on their way to Lake Superior. The sky and the water are insanely blue. It's a serene landscape.

Fairy-tale islands dot the Canadian wilderness.

We traveled through Hemlo, then Marathon. Marathon has been around only since 1944, when the Marathon Paper Company built its first mill in the area. Among the towns along Hwy. 17, this one looked most like a city. Here, the Trans-Canada moves back toward Lake Superior. The weather began to improve considerably as we began tracing the curves of the shoreline.

Along a stretch between Marathon and Terrace Bay, we had our only moose encounter. A female was browsing in a watery ditch alongside the highway. She disappeared into a thicket as we drew near.

As we moved westward, I noticed that the road signs, which had been in English and French, became predominantly English. By the time we reached Thunder Bay the following day, French had disappeared completely. The little rock creatures also seemed to disappear as we moved closer to Superior's farthest northern point.

At Terrace Bay, the land steps down to the lake. The terraces were created by glaciers as they retreated to the north. Each terrace represents the Lake Superior shoreline at a different period of time. Its sandy beach looked like a fun place to hang out and play.

You get to see more of Lake Superior as you travel west on Hwy. 17.

The highway followed the shoreline more closely as we breezed through Schreiber and Rossport. We thought about stopping to see Rainbow Falls Provincial Park, but it looked like a rough, unpaved road, so we continued on along Nipigon Bay.

Nipigon is the northernmost bay on Lake Superior, and nearby Nipigon Lake serves as a put-in point for many wilderness canoe trips. If you're into fishing, Nipigon is a great place for charter fishing trips, either on Lake Superior or inland. Hiking trails are abundant also.

After a day of motorcycle touring, we were happy to stop in our tracks at the Northland Inn. Too tired to get back on the bike and explore downtown, we settled for an uninspired supper at the nearby BP station. (It's now an Esso station.) We would have done better at the Nipigon Drive-in, which featured hamburgers and poutine (cheese curds covered with gravy). We stopped at the little red-and-white hamburger stand after dinner and ordered ice cream cones which we ate before we dragged ourselves back to our room and crashed.

Nipigon to Grand Marais

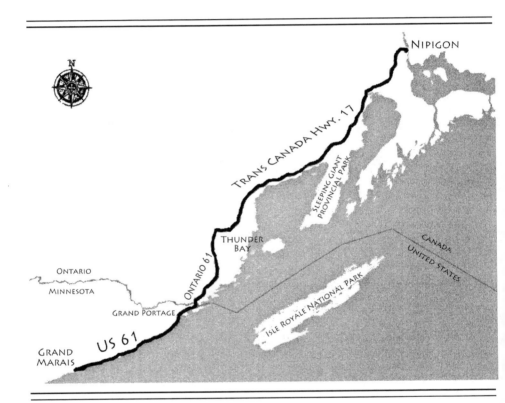

Inuksuk

I saw the first one shortly after we passed the turnoff for Wawa. It stood near the top of a high bluff. Made of the same red rock as the bluff, it almost disappeared into its surroundings. It was just a pile of stones . . . with a vaguely human shape.

As we drove deeper into the Michipicoten First Nations reservation, the land took on a quiet, brooding look. Tall pines lined the road and rimmed lakes. I began to see more of the rock figures as we entered the more isolated part of Ontario. Lake Superior was somewhere off to our left as the Trans-Canada Highway turned more sharply inland. Pukaskwa National Park stood between us and the lake, with a single dirt road leading from the highway into the park.

Sometimes there was only one rock cairn along the highway. Sometimes there would be a group of three or more, as if they had gathered

No inuksuk in Grand Marais, Minnesota.

for a party. Most of them looked slightly, eerily human. I tried to grab a photo or two as we passed, but the camera couldn't see what my eyes could zoom in on in an instant.

When we stopped, I asked Ralph if he had seen them. He said he had learned about them during a five-hundred-mile canoe trip to Hudson's Bay that he took with the YMCA in his junior year of high school. "The Indians make them to show you the way to go," he said, "like blazes in a forest."

Some post-trip research revealed that *inuksuit* (the plural of *inuksuk*) are scattered from Alaska to Greenland. The rock forms were/are used by the Inuit as beacons to guide travelers and hunters, pointing them to specific landmarks or game-hunting areas. The humanoid beacons we saw on the Trans-Canada were most likely what the Inuit call *innunguaq*, "pretend Inuk", built by tourists. More than ninety of them have been counted along the way. Rangers in some of Canada's national parks have pulled down inuksuit built in the parks because they confuse park visitors about the actual paths to follow.

As we moved away from the reservation, the stone figures became less numerous. By the time we reached Thunder Bay, nary a one marked the highway.

Later, we walked along a rocky portion of lake shore in Grand Marais, Minnesota. We came upon a number of piles of stone. Some of them looked like inuksuit, their creators having recently come through Canada, no doubt. Others seemed to follow the imaginations of their creators, with little or no meaning to them.

An upwardly-mobile young father approached the area with his toddler son. The father was neatly dressed in khaki shorts and a golf shirt. His hair was impeccably styled. He asked his son, "Do you want to make a rock sculpture?"

The spell of the inuksuk was broken.

Grand Marais to US 53

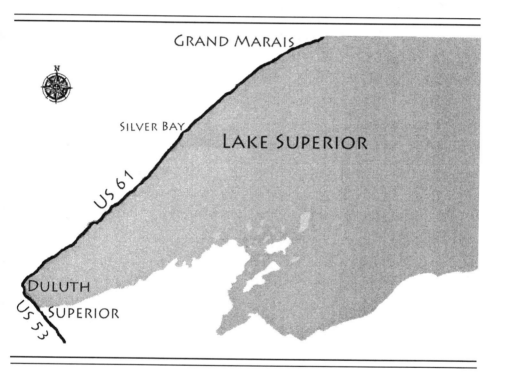

The memorial to Terry Fox is a peaceful place for a rest stop.

Home Again

We started down the wolf's long nose in the morning, after grabbing a quick breakfast at Tim Horton's across the highway from the hotel. Horton's is the Starbucks of Canada, and the coffee was a good eye-opener.

The air was clean and the sun shone brightly in an almost cloudless sky. From Nipigon, Hwy. 17 runs concurrently with Ontario Hwy. 11. As we neared Thunder Bay, the road widened to four lanes and became an expressway. A long-term road-widening project was operating alongside the highway. Clearly, more traffic lanes were coming to the area.

We stopped north of Thunder Bay to drive up a hillside to a memorial for Terry Fox. Fox was a one-legged runner who attempted to run across Canada to fund cancer research. Unfortunately, he was struck down by the disease before completing his journey. The monument is gorgeous, made of bronze, and placed on a 45-ton slab of granite surrounded by amethyst geodes. It overlooks Lake Superior, and it offers a wonderful place to rest and stretch your legs.

Out in Lake Superior, the Sleeping Giant reposed. A rocky peninsula that sticks out into the lake and forms the bay of Thunder Bay, it looks like a sleeping man. The Ojibwe called him Nanaboujou, the shape-shifting trickster rabbit. It's one of Canada's Seven Wonders, and it offers sweeping views of the lake and the city.

As we neared Thunder Bay, we passed the Amethyst Mine Panorama. If you're a rock hound, or you just like amethysts, it's a good place to stop. The mine encloses North America's largest amethyst deposit, and amethyst is the official gemstone for the province of Ontario. For $3 per pound, you can dig your own amethysts to take home. Admission is $8 each.

Thunder Bay also houses Fort William Historical Park, a living history site that re-creates the days of the Canadian fur trade. Forty-seven reconstructed buildings and re-enactors tell the story of the trading post on the Kaministiquia River. It's a great trip back through time. There's also an astronomical observatory that's open Thursday through Saturday. You can also camp there.

As we passed through the city and back into the countryside, I was struck by the presence of farms along the way. I equate the area with the great North Woods, not farm country. I remembered a saying my I heard from my father: "If the house is in good repair and the fields aren't, the woman's in charge. If the fields are well managed but the house is run down, the man is in charge." Gazing at the farms as we sailed past, it was hard to tell who was in charge. Maybe it was an equal partnership.

Stop and enjoy the scenery at the overlook south of Ryden's store.

We crossed the Kaministiquia River and Hwys. 17 and 11 turned west toward Manitoba. We began traveling southwest on Ontario 61, which narrowed to two lanes. We passed a truck hauling logs, which reminded me of childhood trips to the North Woods. A sign along the highway told us we had crossed back into the Central Time Zone. We soon crossed the Pigeon River and returned to the United States and Minnesota.

In due course, we began seeing signs alerting us to the Grand Portage port of entry. One said, "NO PHOTOS." I obediently put my camera in my jacket pocket, though I was tempted to take photos just because I was told I couldn't.

The entrance to the station at Grand Portage is very plain, with barely a sign of welcome. Michigan, on the other hand, had a big sign that said "Welcome to the United States" in big, bold letters.

There wasn't another vehicle within miles of us. Nevertheless, the border patrol agent decided to pull us over for a random check. He told us our bike was the lucky tenth vehicle to cross that morning. Somehow, I doubted it.

We surrendered our passports so he could compare them to a computer database in the office. When he returned, the agent asked the usual questions. "What were you doing in Canada?" "Do you have anything to declare?" He had us open up our saddle bags. He scrutinized the tools Ralph carries in case he needs to do a little motorcycle maintenance, then sent us on our way.

If you need to exchange Canadian money for U.S. dollars, you may want to do it at Ryden's Border Store just south of the border station. Local banks don't offer this service. However, many businesses in Grand Marais accept Canadian loonies just as if it's U.S. currency.

A few miles south of Ryden's is a scenic overlook. It's one of many on Minnesota's North Shore and the view is well worth a stop. In fact, in Minnesota, you can see more of Lake Superior than you can almost anywhere else along the Circle Route. It almost makes up for the rough pavement up ahead. The road from the border to Grand Marais is the victim of some of the worst road maintenance we encountered during the entire trip, even the designated "rough road" in Ontario.

The annual powwow and rendezvous was in full swing at the Grand Portage National Monument. Run by the National Park Service, the monument explains the history of the Ojibwe people – the first people to settle in this area -- and the fur trade. The Indians called the footpath between the Pigeon River and Lake Superior the "Great Carrying Place," which

French fur traders translated as Grand Portage. Natives and voyageurs used the portage to get around rapids and falls on the river and deliver their ninety-pound bundles of fur to the trading post on the lake's edge. The trail connected the Northwest Company post at Lake Superior with Fort Charlotte, a fur-trading depot nine miles inland.

Admission to the national monument is free; however, donations are accepted. Camping at the monument is limited to 10 persons. You can make a reservation request at www.nps.gov/grpo. The site also has a gift shop where you can buy a patch for your jacket.

If you'd rather not sleep on the hard ground, the Grand Portage band of the Ojibwe operates the nearby Grand Portage Lodge and Casino.

Southwest of Grand Portage, US 61 sticks to the curves of the Lake Superior shoreline like Velcro. The water is nearly always in sight. You can look out over the shimmering inland "ocean" and see lakers and salties as they steam to and from the Duluth harbor. The air is freshened by the water and the scent of towering pines. This is Minnesota's seacoast.

Half-way between Grand Portage and Grand Marais is the Naniboujou Lodge. Situated where the Brule River enters Lake Superior, this once was a private club. It's now a resort and is on the National Register of Historic Places. You'll realize why when you see the lodge's distinctive Art Deco and Cree Indian interior—not to mention the bright red trim on the outside.

Also on the Brule is Judge C.R. Magney State Park, one of several state parks along the North Shore. Judge Magney was instrumental in establishing 11 state parks in Minnesota. If you're looking for a place to stop and hike or camp, Magney has much to offer, including a series of waterfalls.

After passing though the tiny towns of Hovland, Covill and Croftville, we saw a large rock formation out in the lake. It's called Five-Mile Rock because it's five miles from Grand Marais. Old-time sailors used to use it as a navigational aid. The next thing we noticed is a little church in Chippewa City, once a village just above Grand Marais. The church, St. Francis Xavier Catholic Church, is built of hand-hewn and dove-tailed logs and is all that remains of the village. It is undergoing restoration.

It was lunch time and our Tim Horton's breakfast had worn off. We decided to eat at the Gun Flint Tavern in Grand Marais. Housed in the old Grand Marais State Bank Building, the Gun Flint has been serving craft brews and organic food since 1998. It's as much of a symbol of the artist-colony Grand Marais as the bank was of the lumber-industry Grand Marais. We decided over beer that a week of intense bike-riding was catching up to us.

After lunch we walked down Wisconsin St. to the Harbor Inn and booked a room. We parked the Victory in front of the motel, which faces the lake. Like much of Grand Marais, the family-owned Harbor Inn has been updated. Our room was recently redecorated in a pale blue and navy nautical scheme and very comfortable.

A pair of Victories share parking space in Grand Marais.

Joyne's Department Store is Grand Marais' shopping anchor, selling everything from beach balls to pots and pans to hiking boots. We toured the local organic grocery store and wondered what the lumberjacks would have thought about it. Ralph picked up a Lake Superior Circle Tour patch for his jacket at the Lake Superior Trading Post. I purchased a painting done on birch bark at the Eight Broadway Gallery. We spent the rest of the day hanging out in the harbor, looking at the lake and soaking up the sun like a pair of turtles.

We grabbed a couple of slices of pizza at Sven and Ole's for dinner, then walked back to the motel. Another Victory – a more recent model – had parked next to ours. Although Victory has been taking some market share away from Harley-Davidson, Harleys still outnumber Victories on the road. Ralph and the owner, who was from the state of Washington, spent some time comparing notes.

The following morning we were back on the road again, climbing the hill out of Grand Marais toward Duluth. We breezed past Cascade River State Park, the North Shore Commercial Fishing Museum in Tofte, and Temperance River State Park, intent on finishing our tour.

At nearby Schroeder, there's a sign for Father Baraga's Cross. It's easy to miss. It's on the left side of Hwy. 61 as you head south. Down a short paved road is a granite cross that commemorates the wooden cross Father

Leaving Grand Marais

Frederic Baraga planted here in 1846 after a rough and stormy crossing from Madeline Island in a canoe. It was the beginning of missionary work in northeastern Minnesota. The river where he landed is the Cross River.

Still hugging the lake, Hwy. 61 brought us to Temperance River State Park. Taconite Harbor soon came into view, its black loading docks jutting out into the lake, ready to send ore carriers laden with taconite pellets east toward the St. Lawrence Seaway. Taconite Harbor is a ghost town now. The last family left the area in 1988 and shipping from the docks ceased in 2001. The Minnesota Department of Natural Resources has designated the area as a harbor of refuge for small boats.

Tettegouche State Park is known for being the home of the High Falls, where the Baptism River drops 60 feet on its way to Lake Superior. Once a private camp, it has an area filled with early twentieth-century log buildings, which have been placed on the National Register of Historic Places. We swooshed on by the park and through the mining town of Silver Bay toward Split Rock Lighthouse.

If you've never visited Split Rock Lighthouse, I urge you to do so. The octagonal yellow brick 1910 light is perhaps the prettiest on the lake, and the Minnesota Historical Society does a great job of telling its story. Along with the nearly adjacent Gooseberry Falls State Park., it's one of the most-visited sites in Minnesota.

In 1994, the Minnesota Department of Transportation took some of the fun out of riding the North Shore when it completed a pair of tunnels at Silver Cliff Creek, just before the entrance to Two Harbors. The tunnels eliminated a couple of cliff-hanging hairpin turns that made even a car ride thrilling. If you like to hear the rumble of your motorcycle, the tunnel is a good place to give the throttle a little rip.

At the southwest end of Two Harbors, US 61 presents you with a choice. You can take the I-35 expressway into Duluth, or the slower, more scenic route. We stayed on 61, which is re-named North Shore Drive. It passes places to buy smoked fish (a local delicacy), old mom-and-pop resorts and some very nice lakefront homes. We crossed the Knife and Lester Rivers and found ourselves in Duluth, where the road is re-named London Road.

Huge old mansions line London Road. Once the homes of lumber barons and other entrepreneurs, some are bed and breakfast establishments. One of the most famous is Glensheen, the mansion built by Chester A. Congdon, who made his fortune in iron mining. The University of Minnesota-Duluth operates tours daily from 9 a.m. to 4 p.m. Glensheen is at 3300 London Road. Order tickets in advance at **https://glensheen. wp.d.umn.edu**.

We wanted to ride Duluth's scenic Skyline Parkway, which crosses the city from east to west and offers spectacular views of the lake. However, floods from the previous year had damaged many of the streets along the route. After several detours, we gave up and wound our way into downtown Duluth, where we picked up US 2. We crossed the Richard I. Bong Memorial Bridge into Wisconsin. Bong was a World War II ace who shot down more than 40 enemy planes.

From the bridge, it was a short distance to US 53. We had reached the tip of the wolf's nose. The circle was complete.

The Bong Memorial Bridge marked the end of the ride.

The best Lake Superior scenery is along Minnesota's North Shore.

Fun Facts about Lake Superior

Lake Superior is about 10,000 years old.

It is the largest freshwater lake in the world by surface area and third largest in volume. It has a surface area of 31,700 miles.

It holds 3 quadrillion gallons, enough to cover North and South America with a foot of water. It can hold all of the water of all the Great Lakes, plus three additional Lake Eries.

More than 300 streams and rivers empty into Lake Superior. There are at least forty-two major waterfalls around the lake.

The lake is 350 miles long and 160 miles across. The length of the shoreline is 1,826 miles. The "official" Lake Superior Circle Tour is approximately 1,300 miles.

The Canadian side of the lake rises about 18 inches per century. This is because the land is "bouncing back" after the retreat of the last glacier 10,000 years ago.

Approximately 550 shipwrecks are known to have occurred on Lake Superior.

Lake Superior received its name from early French explorers who described its location as "above" or "superieur" to Lake Huron. The Indians called it Gitchee Gumee, "big water".

Superior's average water temperature is 40 degrees F.

Sources

I don't ride around with an encyclopedia in my head. In addition to my personal experiences, I consulted the following sources for this book.

Bogue, Margaret Beattie, *Around the Shores of Lake Superior, a Guide to Historic Sites*, second edition, University of Wisconsin Press, 2007

Molloy, Lawrence J., *A Visitor's Guide to the Historic Quincy Mine*, Great Lakes Geoscience, LLC, Ontonagon, Michigan, 2007

Romig, Walter, L.H.D., *Michigan Place Names*, Wayne State University Press, 1986

http://ridelakesuperior.com

http://www.seagrant.umn.edu/superior/facts

http://www.lakesuperiorcircletour.info

http://www.midwestweekends.com

http://www.northernontario.travel

About the Author

Cynthia Lueck Sowden is a native of Minneapolis, Minnesota. A graduate of the University of Minnesota School of Journalism and Mass Communications, she worked for many years in corporate communications, public relations and advertising. Her husband, Ralph, is an electrical engineer. They live in Minneapolis.

Cynthia Lueck Sowden has authored three books and contributed to others.

Other Books by Cynthia Lueck Sowden

An Anniversary to Remember: Years One to Seventy-Five (2014, Homegrown Communications)

Ride Minnesota: 23 Great Motorcycle Rides in the North Star State (2013, Homegrown Communications)

Wedding Occasions: 101 New Party Themes for Wedding Showers, Rehearsal Dinners, Engagement Parties and More! (1990, Brighton Publications)

To order, visit **www.mnride.net**.

Made in the USA
San Bernardino, CA
01 October 2015